Help Me Find My Painting!

Cindy Prince

Book 2: Sir Peter Paul Rubens

Hi there!

My name is Frencesca, and this is my little sister Isabella.

One minute, we were admiring our new baby brother, and the next, we were here!

If we give you clues...

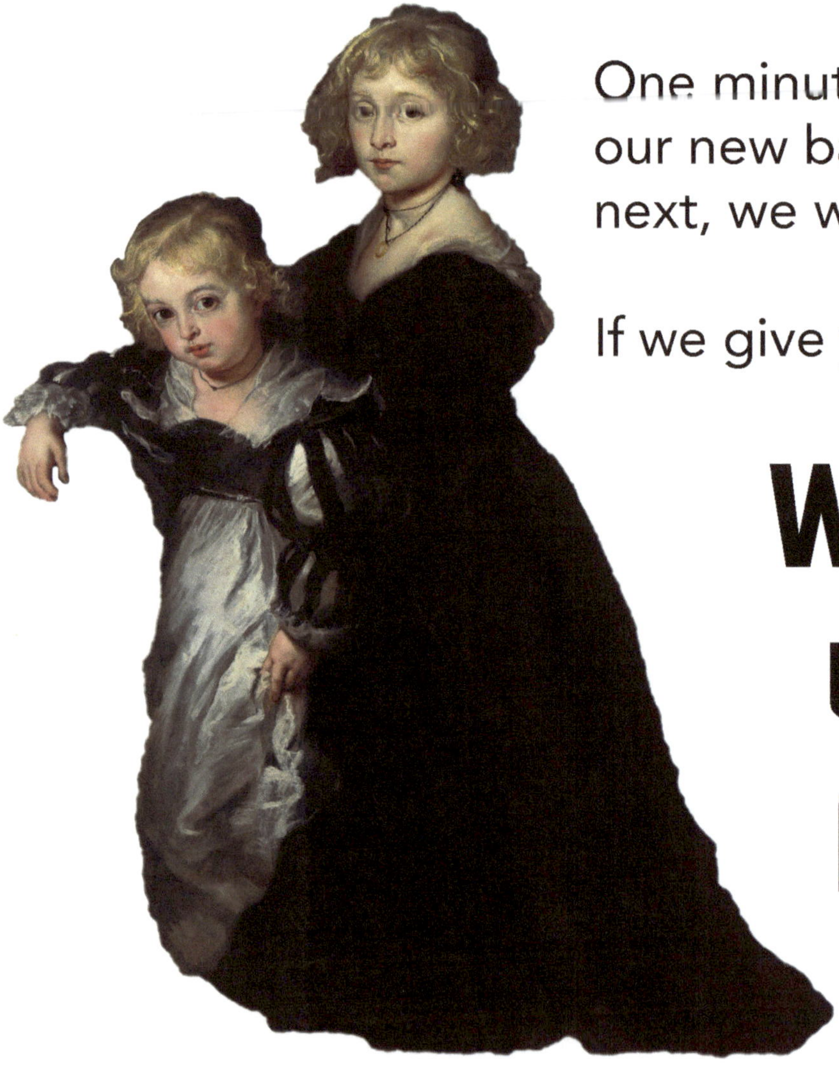

Will you help us find our painting?

Our family was painted by Sir Peter Paul Rubens in 1630. He was living with us as an emissary to the King during the Thirty-Years War!

Finding our painting is going to be tricky.

Look closely at Isabella's dress.

Do you see how extravagent and detailed it is?

Baroque art has LOTS of ornaments and frills!

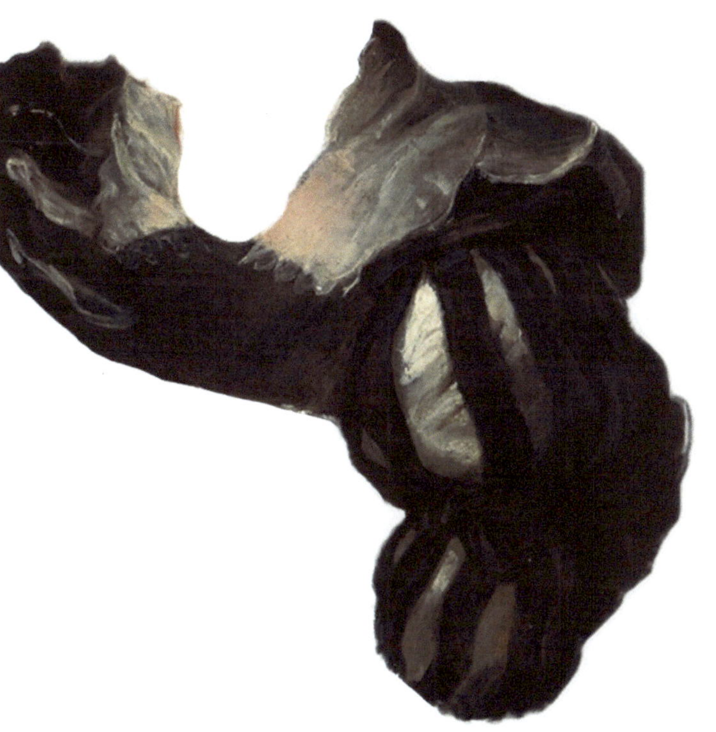

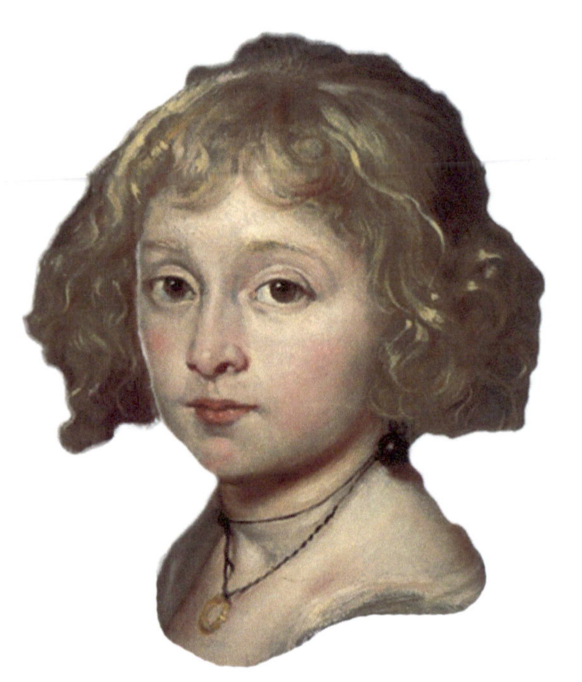

Now look at the expression on my face.

Do you see how I'm looking right at you? My expression is meant to draw you into the picture!

What do you think I'm feeling?

My painting is meant to look physically and emotionally real!

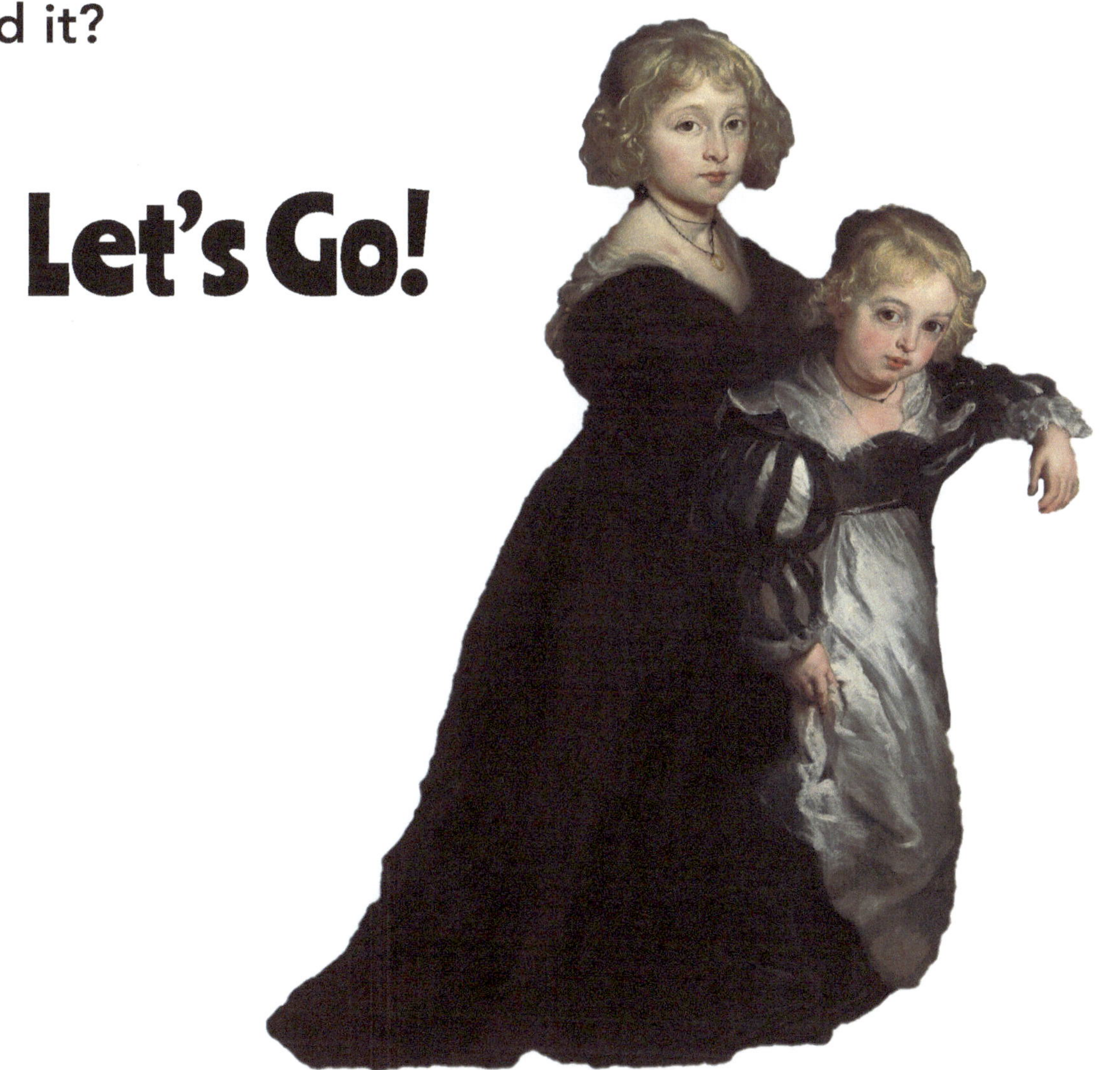

Do you think you can
find it?

Let's Go!

Is this my painting?

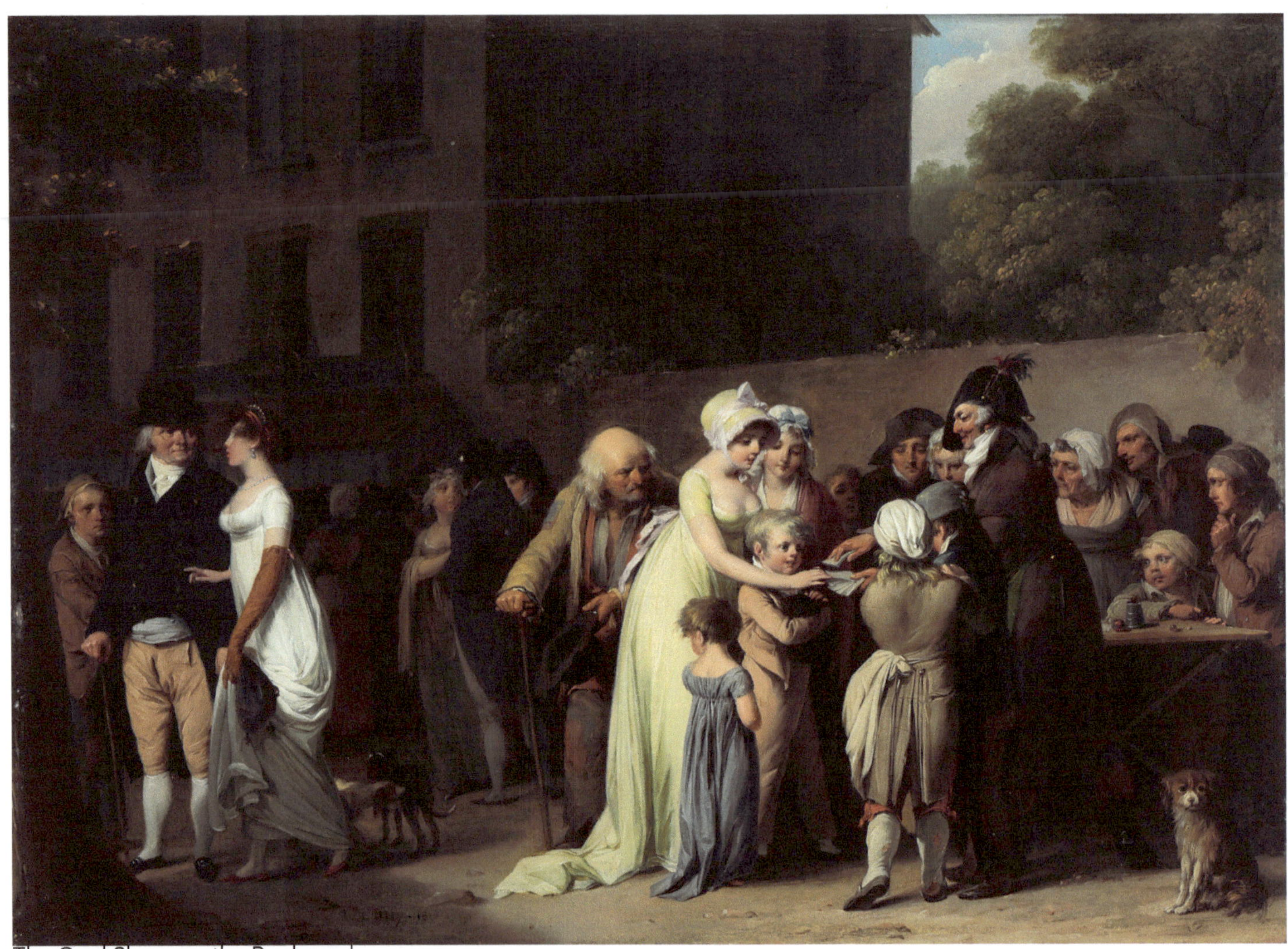
The Card Sharp on the Boulevard

What do you think?

No!

Why not?

Because their clothes are ordinary!

Do you see how there aren't many ornaments or frills?

This is what people would wear normally around town in Paris a long time ago.

Is this my painting?

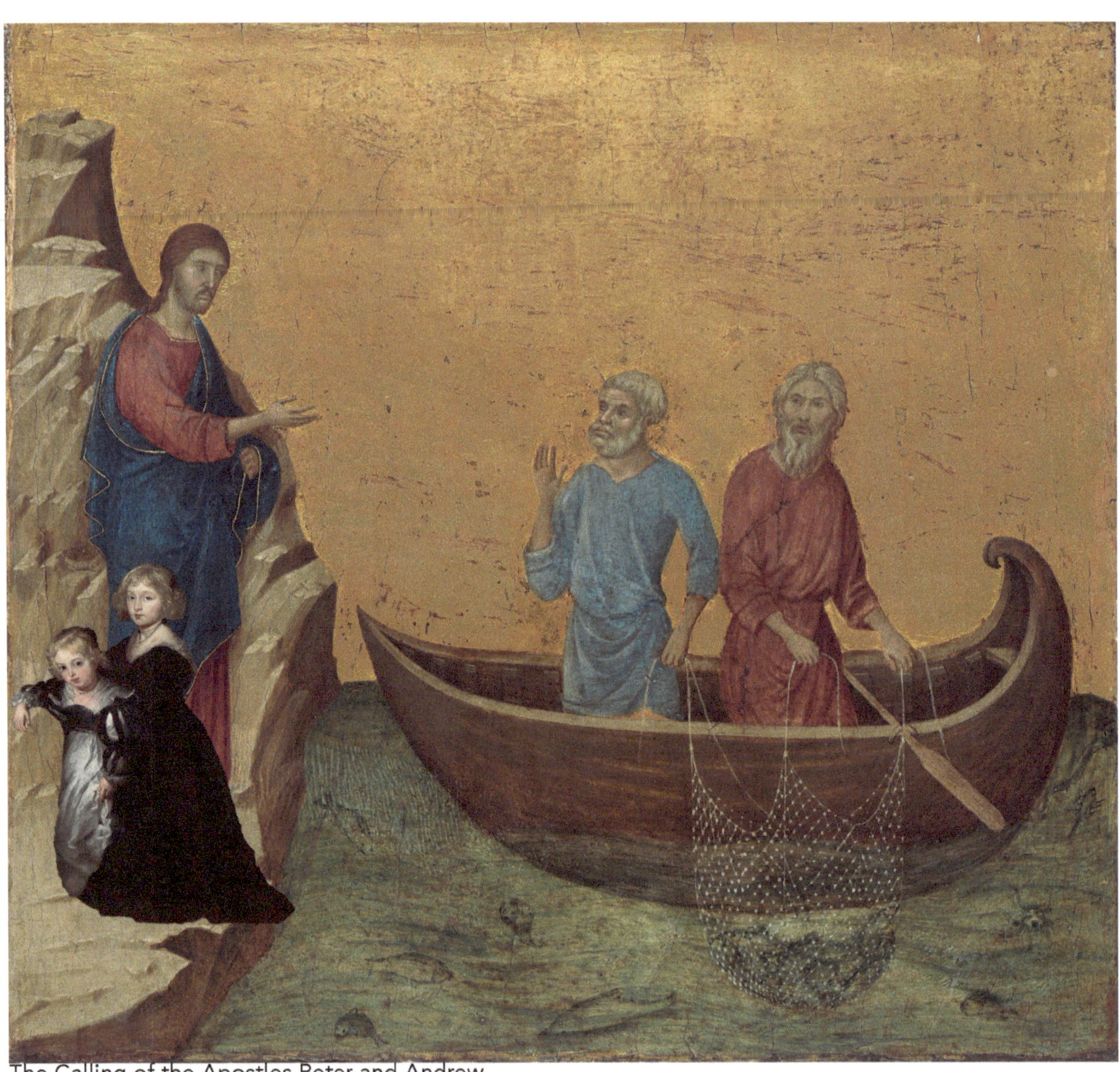

The Calling of the Apostles Peter and Andrew

What do you think?

No!

Why not?

The style is visually distinct because this is a painted panel, not canvas!

This is also a story from the Bible, not something the artist saw in real life.

Is this my painting?

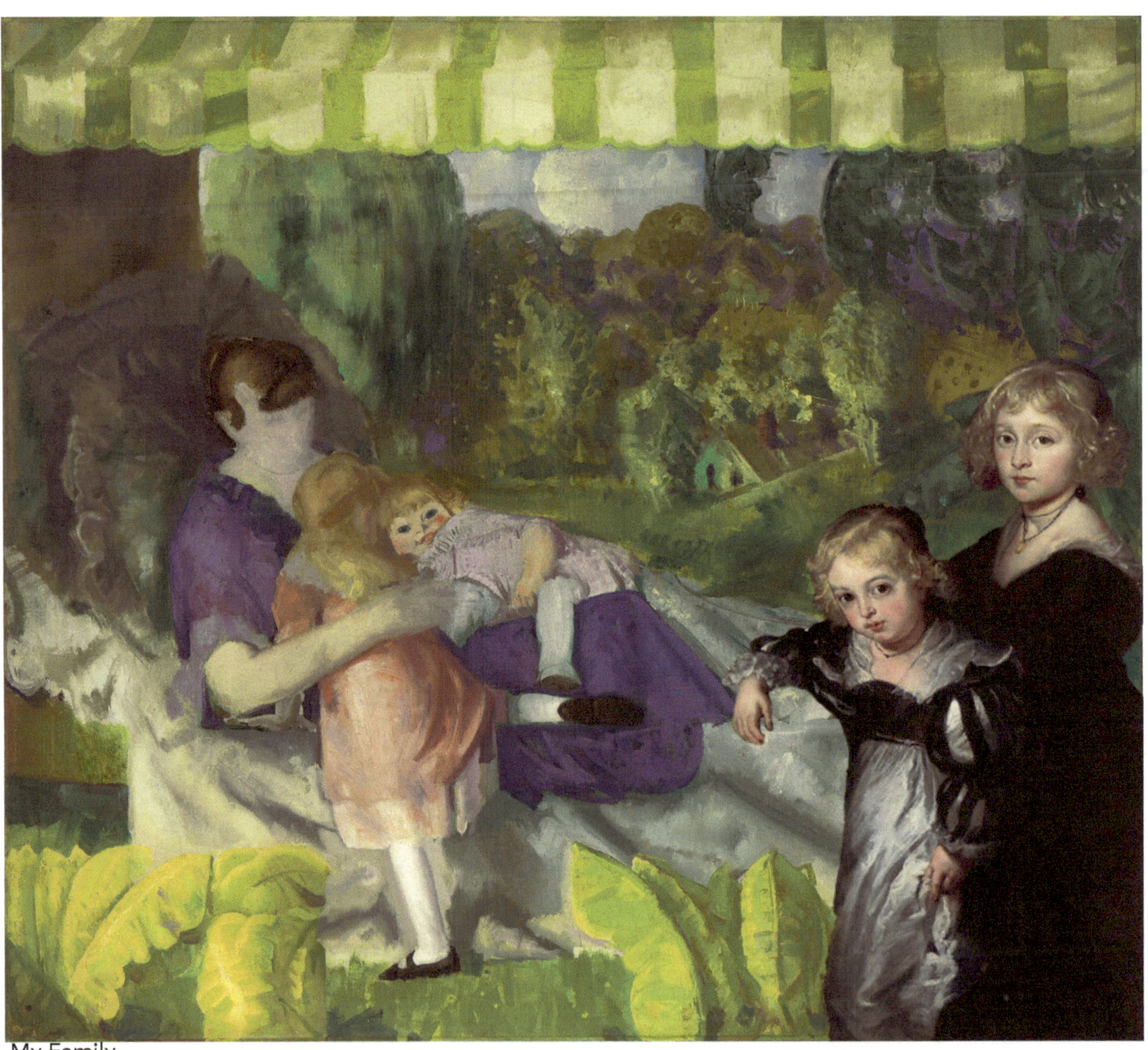

My Family

What do you think?

No!

Why not?

This painting is missing the realistic details and expressions in our painting!

Do you notice how bright the colors are compared to us?

What's your favorite color you can see?

Is this my painting?

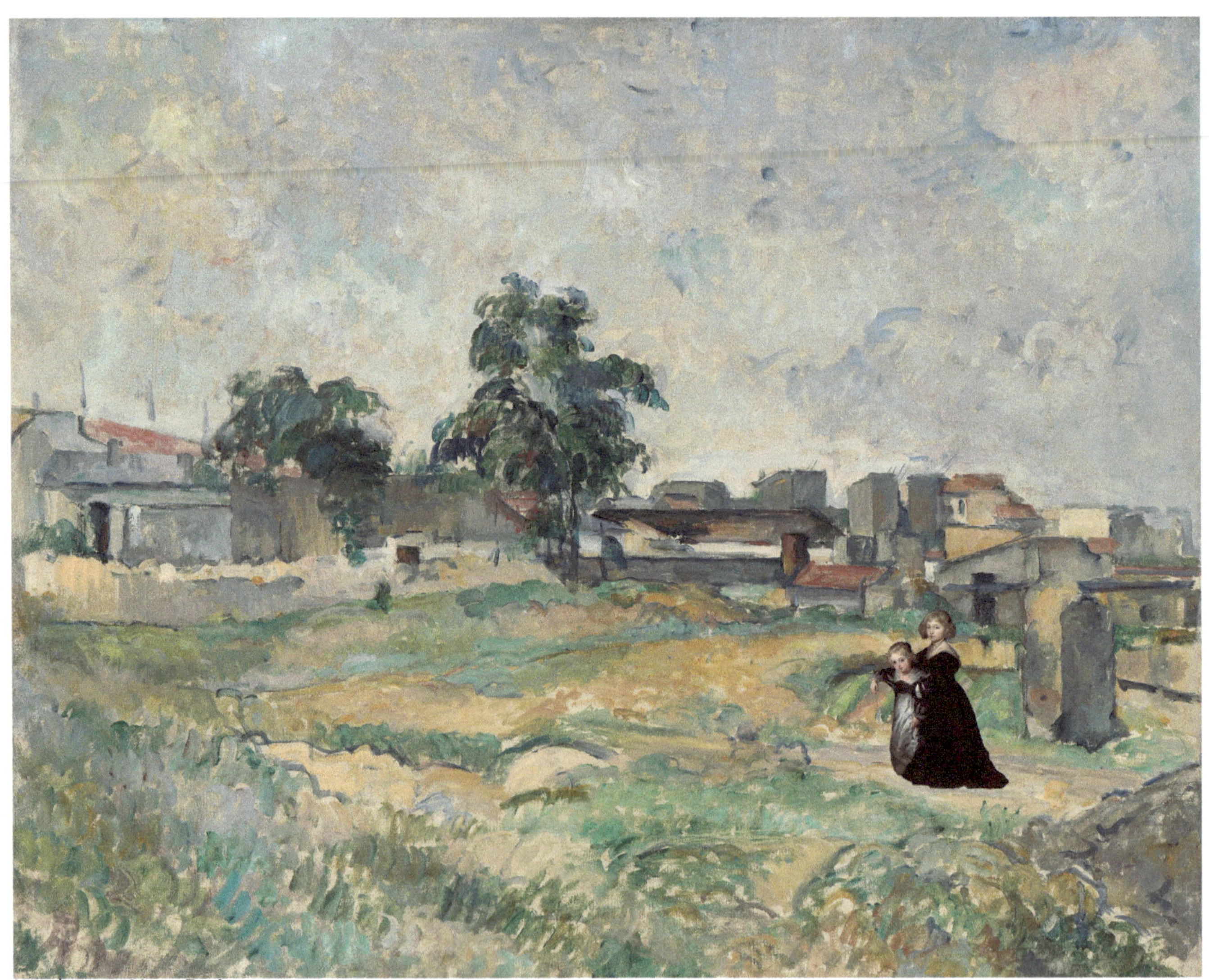

Landscape Near Paris

What do you think?

No!

Why not?

This painting is a landscape. That means there aren't any people in it.

Isabella loves the tall trees!

Do you see how the artist used small brush strokes in different colors to create the image?

Is this my painting?

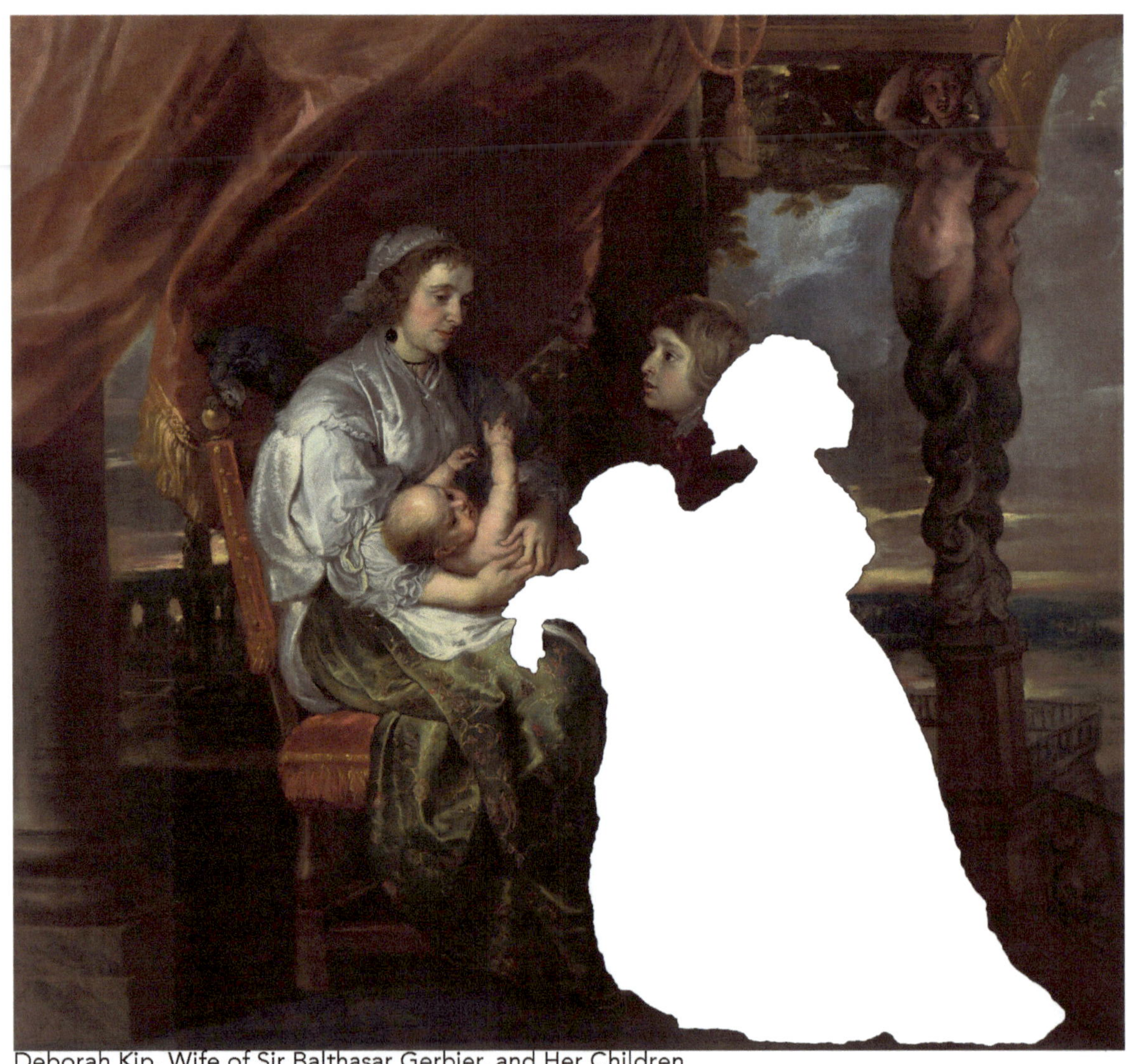

Deborah Kip, Wife of Sir Balthasar Gerbier, and Her Children

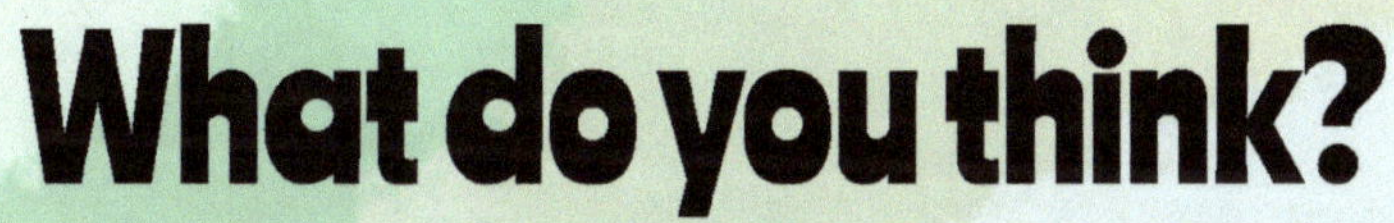
What do you think?

Yes!

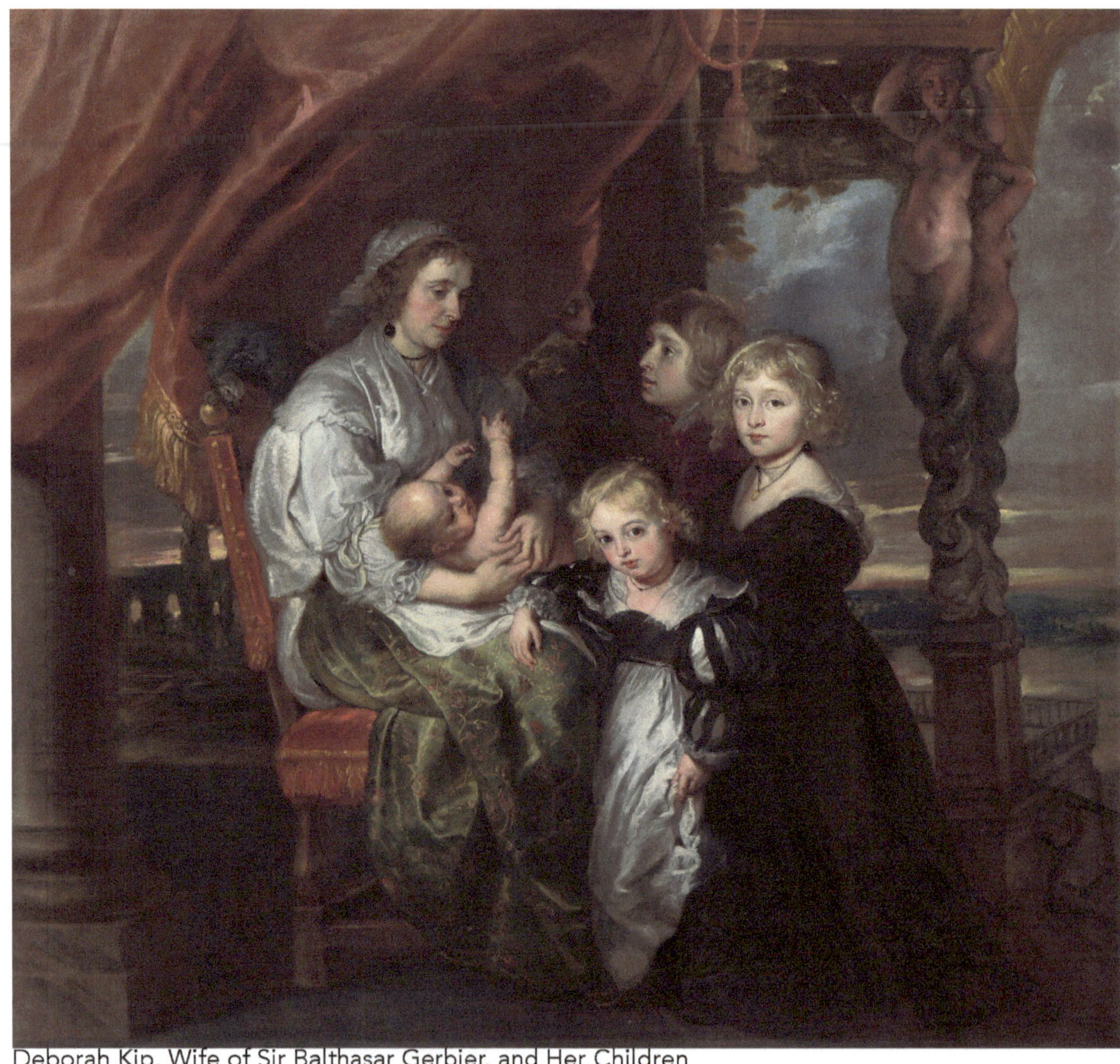

Deborah Kip, Wife of Sir Balthasar Gerbier, and Her Children

You helped me find my painting!

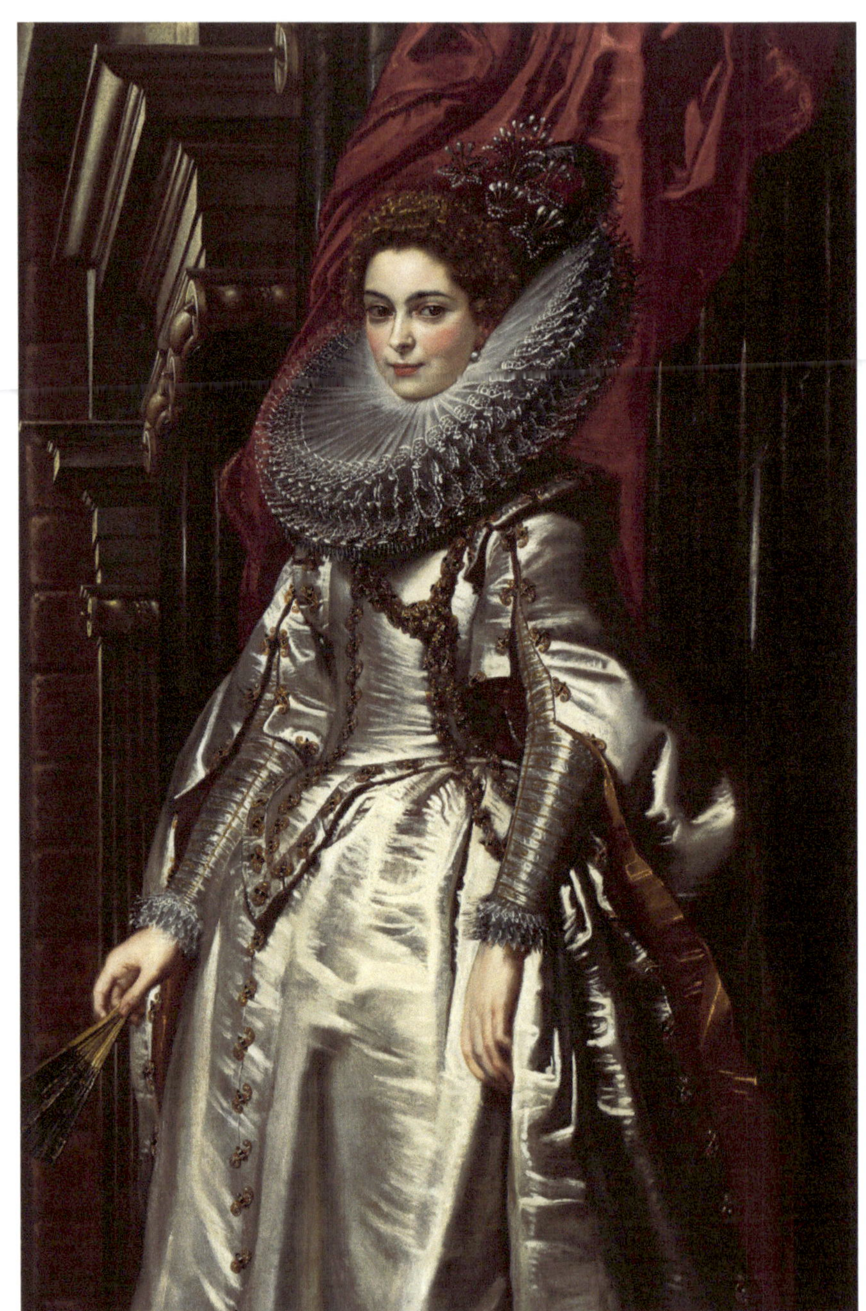

Marchesa Brigida Spinola Doria

Sir Peter Paul Rubens

He is considered the most influential artist of the Flemish Baroque tradition.

He emphasized movement, color, and sensuality in his art.

Did you know he was also a cartoonist, scholar, and a diplomat? Sir Rubens was also very committed to his wife and children.

He painted diverse subjects, including stories from history, mythology, and scripture.

Besides flourishing details, Baroque artists used light and dark to make their paintings striking and dramatic. Can you see that in the next two paintings?

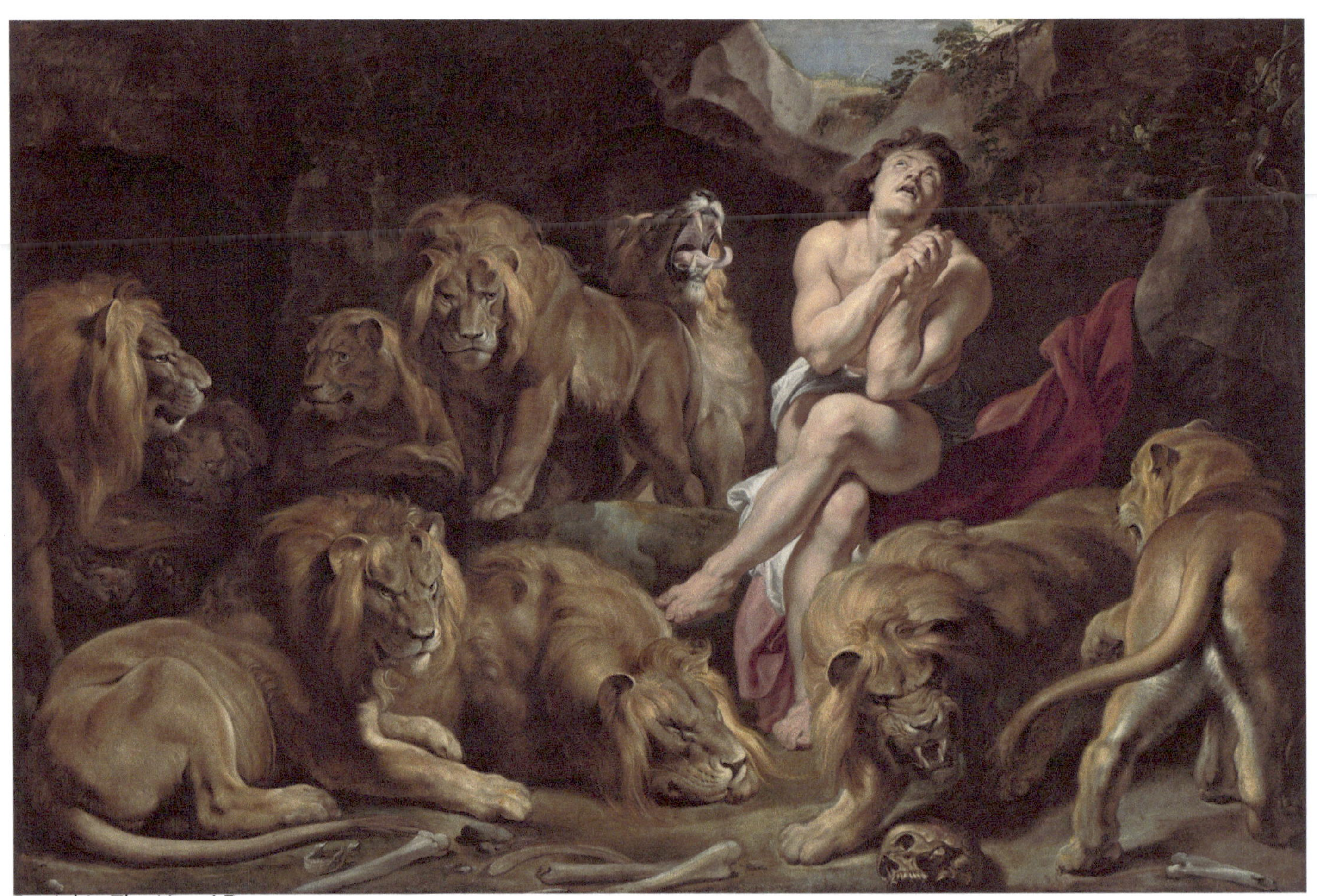

Daniel In The Lions' Den

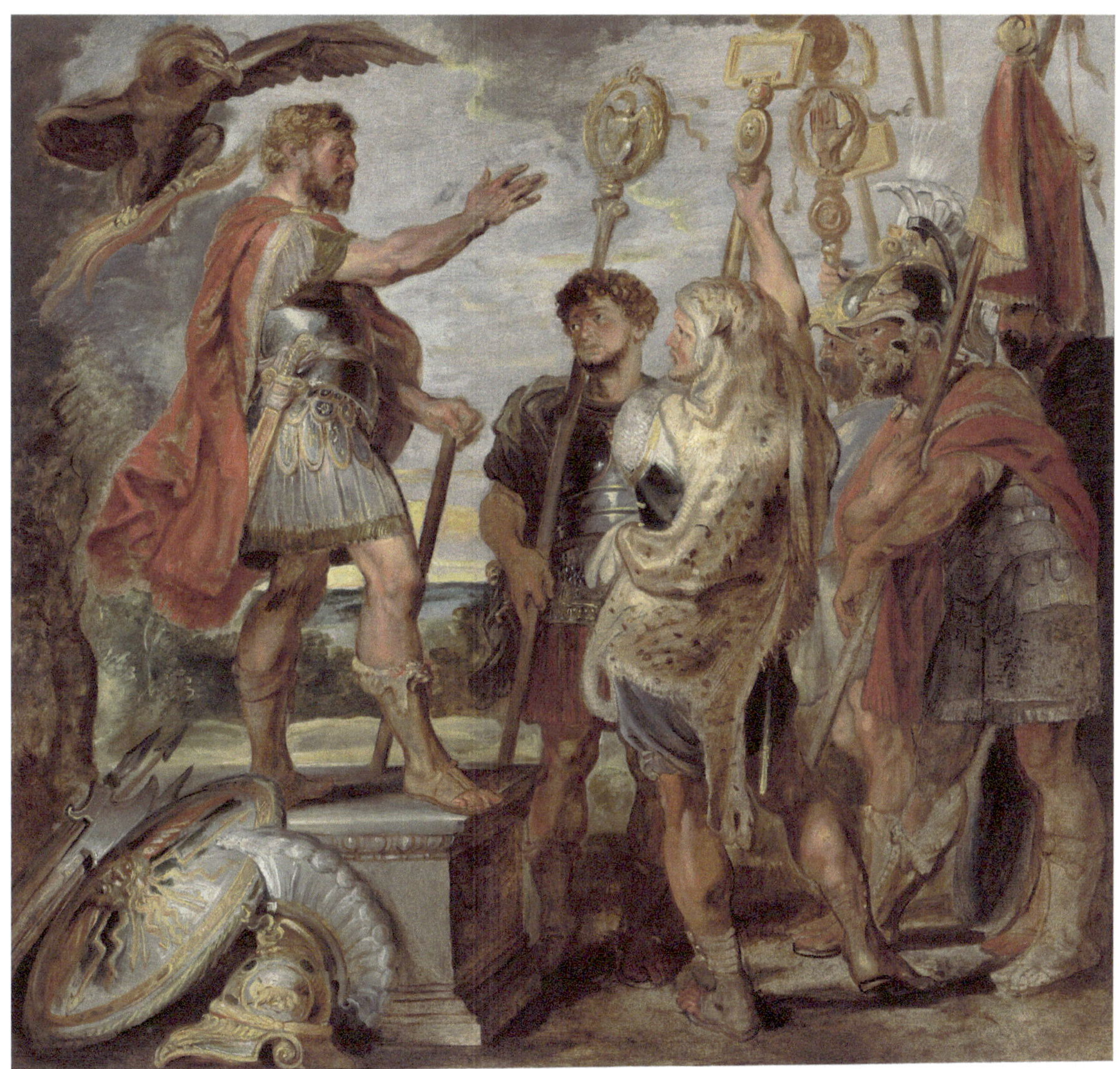

Decius Mus Addressing the Legions

Sir Peter Paul Rubens

Flemish, 1577 - 1640

Peter Paul Rubens was born in Siegen, Westphalia, on 28 June 1577. He was named after Saints Peter and Paul, on whose feast day he was born. His father, Jan Rubens (d. 1587), was a lawyer and magistrate from Antwerp who, because of his Calvinist faith, had fled the Spanish-occupied city and moved to Cologne in 1568 with his wife, Maria Pypelinckx (d. 1608). Jan Rubens was banished to Siegen in 1577 because he had an affair with the wife of Willem of Orange, leader of the Dutch revolt against Spain. Rubens' mother remained with her husband, and after his death she returned to Antwerp with Rubens and his older brother, Philip (1574-1611).

Rubens converted to Catholicism and entered the Latin school of Rombout Verdonck, where he received training in the classics. He also worked as a page for a nobleman, an experience that probably taught him the courtly manners that were so important for his future career. Rubens became a master in the Antwerp Saint Luke's Guild in 1598 after a period of training with three different teachers: his distant relative Tobias Verhaecht (1561-1631), Adam van Noort (1562-1641), and Otto van Veen (c. 1556-1629). Van Veen's classicizing style and interest in emblematic literature were particularly important for the young artist.

Rubens left for Italy in 1600 and remained there until 1609. He quickly entered into service with Vincenzo Gonzaga, Duke of Mantua. It is not certain how he attained this position, but he may have been recommended by Van Veen, who, as court painter to the Spanish governor in Antwerp, Archduke Albert, and his wife, Isabella, would probably have met the duke in 1599 when he visited the city. In Mantua Rubens painted a number of portraits of the ducal family, but of greater consequence was the opportunity to study and make copies of the artistic treasures in the Gonzaga Collection, among them frescoes by Andrea Mantegna and Giulio Romano (c. 1495-1546) and Raphael's cartoons for the tapestry series of the Acts of the Apostles. Rubens also traveled to churches and palaces in nearby Venice to study works by Titian, Tintoretto, and Veronese.

Even though he was attached to the Gonzaga court, Rubens was allowed to travel extensively and undertake commissions from other patrons. He visited Rome in 1602, where he painted three works for the Church of Santa Croce in Jerusalem, a commission he received from Archduke Albert. While in Rome he was able to study classical sculpture as well as works by Raphael and Michelangelo. In 1603 the duke of Mantua asked Rubens to serve as a cultural envoy to the court of Philip III of Spain. On behalf of his patron, Rubens took a number of official presents, including some paintings, and remained at the Spanish court for eight months. His artistic talents were quickly recognized by the powerful duke of Lerma, for whom he painted an impressive equestrian portrait (Madrid, Museo Nacional del Prado).

Upon his return to Mantua, Rubens received an important commission from Vincenzo Gonzaga: three paintings in honor of the Holy Trinity for the choir of the Jesuit church in Mantua, on which he worked between 1604 and 1605. In 1606 he was in Genoa, where he received commissions for a large altarpiece of the Circumcision for the Jesuit church and several portraits of the Genoese aristocracy, including Marchesa Brigida Spinola Doria (NGA 1961.9.60). During a second stay in Rome (1606-1608), Rubens lived for a while with his older brother, Philip, a promising scholar and jurist. As one of the favorite pupils of Justus Lipsius (1547-1606), Philip was deeply immersed in the neo-Stoic philosophy espoused by his mentor and was instrumental in introducing his brother to a sophisticated circle of humanists, antiquarians, and scientists. Rubens seems to have found his real milieu among these intellectuals but was compelled to leave it behind in October 1608, when he was suddenly called back to Antwerp because of his mother's death.

Rubens returned to Antwerp at a time when the city was experiencing a period of peace and prosperity as a result of the Twelve Years' Truce (1609-1621) with the Dutch republic. His talent and ambitions were quickly recognized, and he soon established a large workshop to assist him in executing his numerous commissions. Rubens often indicated his compositional ideas with drawings and oil sketches, which his assistants reproduced on a larger scale. Many of Rubens' most important compositions were large altarpieces in which he expressed Counter Reformation ideals that had developed after the Council of Trent.

He also established close working relationships with other important masters, including Jan Brueghel the Elder, Frans Snyders, and Jacob Jordaens (1593-1678), and a talented young pupil, Anthony van Dyck. In 1620, for example, Van Dyck assisted Rubens with the execution of ceiling paintings for the Jesuit church in Antwerp.

After Rubens returned to Antwerp, his most important patrons were Archduke Albert and Isabella, who, in 1609, named him court painter and granted him the privilege of living in Antwerp instead of Brussels. During the 1610s he also received commissions for altarpieces from well-known connoisseurs in Antwerp, among them Cornelis van der Geest and Nicolaas Rockox. Among his many commissions from foreign patrons was a tapestry series on the life of Decius Mus, which was ordered by Genoese merchants residing in Antwerp (see Decius Mus Addressing the Legions, NGA 1957.14.2). The duke of Lerma in Spain and Wolfgang William, count Palatine of Neuburg, in Germany were also his patrons. As Rubens' international reputation grew during the 1620s, he received major commissions from, among others, the dowager queen of France, Maria de' Medici, and George Villiers, the duke of Buckingham.

Though Rubens pursued a very active professional life, he was also a dedicated husband and father. In 1609 he married Isabella Brant (see her portrait, NGA 1937.1.47, by Sir Anthony van Dyck), daughter of a prominent burgher and sister of his brother's wife. In 1610 Rubens purchased a large house on the Wapper, near the fashionable promenade of the Antwerp Meir, and, in the course of seventeen years of marriage, their home became one of the most distinguished residences in Antwerp. In 1611 Rubens began an extensive remodeling of the house, creating comfortable living quarters for his family, a spacious studio space, a semicircular gallery inspired by classical architecture to house his growing collection of paintings, sculpture, and curiosities, and an extensive garden. Proclaiming that this house was a temple of art were grisaille paintings on the facade depicting various mythological scenes and a triumphal arch at the entrance to the garden that was crowned with full-length statues of Minerva, goddess of learning, and Mercury, god of elegance and reason. By all accounts, Isabella was an excellent companion and loving spouse, whose unexpected death in 1626 was much lamented by her husband and their two children.

Despite the tragic death of his brother in 1611, Rubens continued to deepen his involvement with classical learning and his contacts with humanist circles throughout Europe. He wrote in Latin, English, French, Italian, and Dutch and maintained extensive correspondence with a number of scholars, notably the antiquarian Nicolas-Claude Fabri de Peiresc. Rubens also collected antique sculpture and cameos. In 1618 he exchanged a number of paintings, including Daniel in the Lions' Den (NGA 1965.13.1), for Sir Dudley Carleton's collection of ancient marbles.

Paralleling Rubens' unrivaled artistic stature in Europe was his increased involvement in politics during the 1620s. After the death of Archduke Albert in 1621, Rubens became a close adviser to Archduchess Isabella in her efforts to establish a stable political environment after the end of the Twelve Years' Truce. Rubens made a number of trips for political purposes, including one to the Dutch republic in 1627 and an extended trip to Spain in 1628. While in Spain, Rubens looked carefully at the Venetian paintings in the Prado and El Escorial and made a number of copies of works by Titian, which greatly influenced his later style of painting. The king of Spain, Philip IV, eventually asked Rubens to serve as a peace mediator between his country and England. Rubens succeeded in his mission and was knighted by the English king, Charles I, for both his political activities and his artistic prowess. While in London from 1629 to 1630, Rubens painted a number of important works for the king, as well as a portrait of the family of Balthasar Gerbier, with whom he had stayed (NGA 1971.18.1).

Shortly after returning to Antwerp in 1630, Rubens married Hélène Fourment, the fifteen-year-old daughter of a prosperous tapestry merchant. Although he continued to serve as adviser to the archduchess until her death in 1633, he did not pursue any more diplomatic missions for her or her successor, Cardinal Infante Ferdinand. In 1635 Rubens acquired the country estate Het Steen, where he spent the last years of his life with his young wife and their children. He painted a number of landscapes during these years that reflect his great love of nature and his awareness of the classical ideals of Arcadian existence most fully expressed in the writings of Virgil.

Rubens died at the end of May 1640 and was buried in the Church of Saint Jacques in Antwerp. A stone tablet in Rubens' memorial chapel is inscribed with an epitaph composed by his friend Jan Caspar Gevaerts:

"Peter Paul Rubens . . . who, among the other gifts by which he marvelously excelled in the knowledge of ancient history and all other useful and elegant arts, deserved also to be called the Apelles, not only of his own age but of all time."

--The National Gallery of Art

Art Citations

Louis-Léopold Boilly. The Card Sharp on the Boulevard. 1806.
    Gift of Victoria and Roger Sant. National Gallery of Art.
    https://www.nga.gov/collection/art-object-page.111638.html

Di Buoninsegna, Duccio. The Calling of the Apostles Peter and Andrew. 1308-1311.
    Samuel H. Kress Collection. National Gallery of Art.
    https://www.nga.gov/collection/art-object-page.282.html

Bellows, George. My Family. 1916.
    Collection of Mr. and Mrs. Paul Mellon. National Gallery of Art.
    https://www.nga.gov/collection/art-object-page.61353.html

Cézanne, Paul. Landscape Near Paris. 1876.
    Chester Dale Collection. National Gallery of Art.
    https://www.nga.gov/collection/art-object-page.46578.html

Rubens, Sir Peter Paul. Deborah Kip, Wife of Sir Balthasar Gerbier, and Her Children. 1629/30.
    Andrew W. Mellon Collection. National Gallery of Art.
    https://www.nga.gov/collection/art-object-page.52457.html

Rubens, Sir Peter Paul. Daniel in the Lions' Den. 1614/1616.
    Ailsa Mellon Bruce Fund. National Gallery of Art.
    https://www.nga.gov/collection/art-object-page.50298.html

Rubens, Sir Peter Paul. Decius Mus Addressing the Legions. 1616.
    Samuel H. Kress Collection. National Gallery of Art.
    https://www.nga.gov/collection/art-object-page.43721.html

Rubens, Sir Peter Paul. Marchesa Brigida Spinola Doria. 1606.
    Samuel H. Kress Collection. National Gallery of Art.
    https://www.nga.gov/collection/art-object-page.46159.html

About the Author

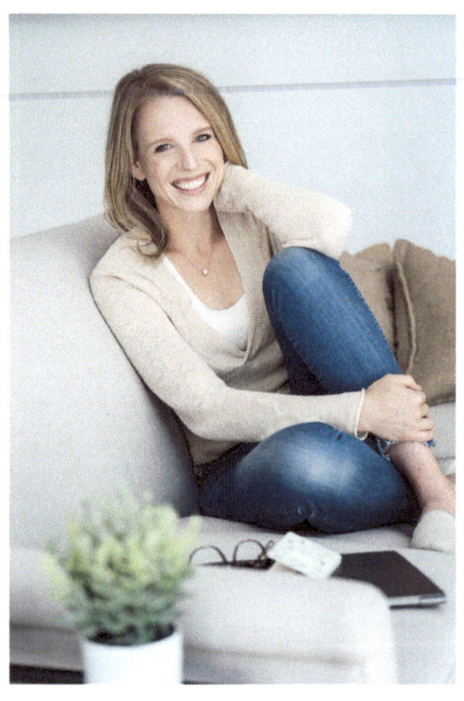

Cindy is first and foremost mother to her four beautiful children and wife to her charming and handsome husband, Scott. She is a musician, a gardener, an athlete, an actor, a lover of Canadian chocolate, and most recently, a writer.

Cindy grew up in Airdrie, AB, Canada, but has lived most of her adult life between California and Colorado. She currently resides in the Denver metro area. Cindy graduated from Brigham Young University in 2005 with a B.S. in Psychology, minoring in Business. She serves actively within her church and community and is always up for a new adventure.

After homeschooling for nine years and having countless discussions with her own four children, Cindy decided to start taking notes. Her picture books are inspired by real conversation and interests with the goal of providing stories that are both fun and helpful for families like her own.

@cindygwrites
www.CindyPrince.com

www.ingramcontent.com/pod-product-compliance
Lightning Source LLC
Chambersburg PA
CBHW042135030726
47599CB00002B/483